REALMS OF MY SOUL II

A Liberating Path

Cocooning with neurodivergent wings

LALI A. LOVE

Disclaimer

The views and poetry expressed in this publication are solely those of the author. The author is not offering the reader medical advice. The messages, suggestions, and philosophies in this book are not meant to be a substitute for seeking professional advice.

Copyright @2023 Lali A. Love

All rights reserved. No part of this book may be reproduced or transmitted in any form or by any means without permission. The author shall have neither liability nor responsibility to any person or entity with respect to any loss, damage, or injury caused or alleged to be caused directly or indirectly by the information contained in this book.

Realms of my Soul II
A Liberated Path

Distributed by Bublish Inc.

eBook ISBN: 978-1-64704-693-4
Paperback ISBN: 978-1-64704-694-1

Award-Winning Publications
Heart of a Warrior Angel: From Darkness to Light (2019)
The Joy of I.T: Infinite Transcendence (2020)
The De-Coding of Jo: Hall of Ignorance (2020)
The De-Coding of Jo: Blade of Truth (2021)
The De-Coding of Jo: Keys to Eternity (2022)
Organic eMotions: Poetry for hUmaNITY (2022)

DEDICATION

To all the children of the sacred light, may you rise in grace knowing your purpose.

COCOONING

There once was an Akashi within,
Whose cosmic song did deeply begin,
Jewels in a net,
Reflecting a set,
Of dewdrops in a web so thin.

Note from the Author

"May my journey inspire many with poetic verse, bringing peace, freedom, and bliss with every word."

Everyone has a story to tell. This is my lyrical account of how I overcame deep emotional wounds to achieve self-actualization and harmony.

I was inspired to release Realms of my Soul, a three-book poetry anthology of my reflections and life lessons as I transitioned from a suffering mindset to a thriving state of being.

I do not have a degree in psychology or claim to provide any professional advice on mental health. My intention is to share my introspection on how I managed anxiety and invisible disabilities over the course of five decades.

Each poem relays my encounters with mental health, disempowering behaviors, embodiment, and mastery.

The second book, A Liberating Path, delves into the healing process and nurturing of the inner child with self-realization, through my neurodivergent perspective and life lessons.

If these poems resonate with your soul, may it stimulate your growth and evolution. May these words incite my readers to transform with an open-heart brimming with joy, to live a harmonious life of purpose, fulfillment, and gratitude.

May you thrive in each aligned moment in coherence, grace, and freedom of expression.

"When we operate from the space of heart-centered consciousness, every Soul becomes our mirror and our teacher. We are all connected within this harmonic web of pure radiant life force energy called Love."
—**Lali A. Love**

Contents

Third Decade: Nurturing my Cocoon 1

Warriors of Light 4
Love Heals 6
Miracle of Life 8
Great Surprise 10
Blossoming Love 12
A Harsh Reality 14
Cards Dealt 16
Emotional Maturity 18
A Mystic's Path 20
Ode to the Thirties 22
The Martyr 24
Fleeting Dream 26
On Autopilot 28
Helicopter Mom 30
Weight of Sorrow 32
Bitter Words 34
Superwoman Complex 36
Precious Art 38
Speaking Direct 40
They Mirror 42
Karmic Broth 44
Uniting the Child 46

Vital Lesson	48
Chronic Illness	50
A Wake-Up Call	52
Heart of a Warrior	54
Insecure Thoughts	56
The Burn Out	58
Power Within	60
Raw Emotions	62
Proverb of Wolves	64
Recycling Doubt	66
Getting Real	68
Expectations	70
Loving Care	72
Acknowledging Triggers	74
Robin's Flight	76
Permission to Feel	78
Spring Cleaning	80
Emotional Currents	82
Becoming the Witness	84
Identity Unmasked	86
Dance of Duality	88
Fostering Sovereignty	90
The Nagging	92
Love of Self	94
White Beams	96
My Daughter's Eyes	98
Knowing my Worth	100
Breaker of Spells	102
Focus of Energy	104
Co-dependency	106

Piercing the Darkness 108
Divergent Minds 110
Solace and Stillness 112

Fourth Decade: Shifting into Purpose 113

Becoming Aware 116
Magic of Love 118
A Lifelong Path 120
The Observer 122
Karmic Points 124
Force of Balance 126
Letting Go 128
Fortitude to Forgive 130
Weary and Worn 132
Twists and Turns 134
Meridian Tapping 136
Resolving the Umbra 138
Vessel of Life 140
Turning Point 142
Building Blocks 144
Improved Creativity 146
Some Good Fun 148
Absolute Acceptance 150
Mindful Downtime 152
Belief System 154
Nature of Spirit 156
Strength of the Warrior 158
Beauty of Imperfection 160
Shadow Integration 162
Present Moment 164

True Essence	166
Emotional Wellness	168
Power of Sleep	170
Coping with Grief	172
In Honour	174
Being Mindful	176
The Haunting	178
Line of Enquiry	180
Trauma Thriver	182
My Truth	184
Setting Boundaries	186
Higher Realms	188
Walking My Path	190
Morning Breaks	192
Guiding Voice	194
Artistic Creation	196
Honouring My Spirit	198
Inner Cave	200
Co-Creating Reality	202
Time Does Fly	204
Coloured Lens	206
State of Flow	208
Melting the Untruth	210
Creating My Legacy	212
About the Author	**213**

A caterpillar, plump and quite slow,
Spins a chrysalis, snug and aglow,
Inside the dark cocoon,
Transformed by its own hand,
Emerges a butterfly, ready to go.

Third Decade: Nurturing my Cocoon

Blossoming love's bliss
Petals open to the sun,
Heart blooms with new life.

In the dark of night,
I find the strength to ignite,
My inner fire bright.

Warriors of Light

I once was lost in darkness, full of doubt,
My soul weighed down by real uncertainty,
But then I saw a glimmer, a flicker of light,
Understanding my true identity.

I learned to love myself just as I am,
To embrace my scars, my unique soul,
Not seeking validation from others,
My worth comes from within, that's my goal.

Now I dance in the flames of my own power,
A shooting star that shines bright in the night,
My destiny unfolds with each passing hour,
And I am unafraid of the challenges in sight.

So, let's all hold our light with might,
And face life with courage, day, and night,
We are warriors of light, ready to fight,
With our hearts beaming bright, forever alight.

World of hurt and pain,
Rise with strength and move beyond,
Love and dreams reveal.

Love Heals

Oh, how the world can be cruel and tough,
With hurt and dreams that seem crushed,
But there's a force that can lift us up,
A power that mends the broken and hushed.

Oh love, you are the light that shines so bright,
The flame that ignites our very soul,
You have the power to heal and unite,
And help us reach our ultimate goal.

You are the force that brings us together,
The glue that binds us as one,
You help us endure the stormy weather,
And guide us until the battle's won.

When we feel lost and all alone,
You are the compass that points the way,
You give us the courage to stand on our own,
And face the challenges that come each day.

Oh love, how you inspire and move us so,
With your gentle touch and tender care,
Your healing power can help us grow,
And give us the strength to persevere.

So let us embrace our force divine,
And let it guide us on our way,
With love in our hearts, we'll surely shine,
And bring a brighter, more hopeful day.

Oh love, you are the light that leads us home,
Our guide, our solace, our very own.

Cherish moments bright,
Parenting teaches essence,
Miracle of life.

Miracle of Life

I cherish the moments, lessons bright,
Parenting brings to my very essence.
The miracle of life reveals insight,
A human history in its essence.

When a little person is created,
Something magical unlocks, it's certain,
Love for them, genuinely, elated,
Divine creation forms as wings unfurl.

Through sleepless nights, tantrums wild,
We nurture with anthems of joy to see.
Whispers of magic to comfort the child,
A rainbow of tales, we conjure with glee.

I pray that life guides them safely through,
Bliss on their path, harmony is the key.
A mother's heart bursting with love so true,
Unwavering adoration, I'd die for thee.

Being a parent is never a burden,
An honor, privilege, to ease the hurting,
My love grows rich, profound, and certain,
Each tender moment, so sweetly soothing.

Connecting to their soul, heartstrings aglow,
I feel their elation, ache, silently quivering,
A mother's heart, fearless, in vibrant show,
For nothing can destroy it, love unerring.

Divine connection,
Message received through their eyes,
New horizon seen.

Great Surprise

I was finally able to build the best family,
Giving affection to my kids, stripped of calamity.
With safety and comforts of a loving home,
They would flourish in harmony within my dome.

I imagined a tale about how they would grow,
When sun beams dappled through my window.
This was my fantasy of their perfect life without woe,
With delight and no strife, flourishing you know?

Trying to relive my youth, they shall nourish my eyes,
Alas an epiphany bloomed, to my great surprise.
My children didn't belong to me, I had to recognize,
Their spirit was on a path of autonomy, no compromise.

I discovered that they were actually teaching me,
Their purity was born to emotionally set free.
This horizon my eyes learned to perceive,
A message of divine connection, I did receive.

Neither my failure nor parental success,
Had the power to change my inner state, no less.

A lighthouse so bright,
Guiding through unending nights,
Revealing secrets.

Blossoming Love

As sunlight bathes the earth golden hue,
A gentle breeze stirs the fragrant air,
So too my heart is roused, for it is true,
That love has bloomed, flowers so rare.

With every passing moment, it grows,
Opens its petals, soft and bright,
Revealing secrets, I had yet to know,
And filling me with joy and delight.

My kids, a lighthouse shining bright,
Guiding me out of my endless night,
I learned to love myself, flaws, and all,
And in doing so, I answered the call.

The call to heal, to grow, to thrive,
To embrace my truth, to come alive,
And as I did, my soul mate did too,
Our love deepened, pure and true.

No longer do I seek to be completed,
For I am whole, my heart fully seated,
In the knowledge that I am enough,
And from this place, it grows tough.

Real devotion isn't about filling a void,
It is two hearts, in harmony, overjoyed,
And accepting each other, as we are,
Two counterparts, shining like a bright star.

So now I walk, heart full and free,
With my soul mate, side by side, happily,
Grateful for the lessons, union, the growth,
And in our love, we will continue to boast.

A parent's shadow,
Haunts the children's early years,
Healing brings new wave.

A Harsh Reality

With every word and action, I thought I knew,
How to raise my little one, pure and true,
But in my quest to guide and shape her way,
I missed the light that made her shine each day.

My heart grew heavy with guilt and pain,
As I saw her spirit begin to wane,
And then it hit me, like a lightning bolt,
That I was repeating my unhealed past, jolt.

My own childhood trauma, projected and raw,
Was seeping into my parenting, like an open sore,
I knew I had to face the pain within,
And let healing begin, so the cycle could end.

It was time to let go of society's lies,
And embrace my child's light, without disguise,
Nurture her essence, and let her be free,
To grow and shine, in her own unique beauty.

So, I acknowledged my inner child, with care,
And began the journey, to heal and repair,
Through the process, my little one bloomed,
Her spirit, her light, forever resumed.

Now I know, with every step and every breath,
That parenting is not about shaping or correcting,
But about guiding and nurturing, with respect,
And letting our little ones, their own path elect.

For in their essence, rests a light so bright,
The unique beauty, that shines like starlight,
And as we embrace and cherish, their true selves,
We create a world, where love always dwells.

Fate once ruled our lives,
Cards dealt, we had to abide.
Destiny's ours.

Cards Dealt

There once was a concept called fate,
The cards we are dealt, we must take.
But destiny is ours,
To fill with our powers,
And create the life we want to make.

Opens eyes to see,
Lessons learned, a brand-new start,
Regret fades with time.

Emotional Maturity

In the depths of my soul, a sorrow lingers,
A mournful ache that my heart still bears.
For once I was lost, a robotic follower,
Heeding stifling systems, ignoring inner layers.

My compliance, a burden I wore with ease,
A passive conformist, I followed blindly.
Suppressing my voice, I bowed to authority,
Neglecting my wisdom, unaware of my agency.

Fearful of questioning, I played a part,
In the discord of 911 terror, world falling apart.
Ignoring my intuition, I stumbled in the dark,
Lost in a system that was tearing me apart.

But one fateful moment, my world was shaken,
As my child's tantrum unleashed the demons.
I saw my shadows, the fangs of the phantom,
I knew the aggression was passed with reason.

In that instant, I broke the cycle of violence,
By embracing my children with loving kindness.
Admitting my mistakes, I vowed to do better,
To honor my child's spirit and unique expression.

Oh, the pain of realization, the weight of regret,
For the time I had lost, the love I had yet to give.
But through my grief, a light shone bright,
A path of growth, of change, of healing in sight.

Here's to the journey of lessons and renewal,
To breaking the chains and living with value.
May this emotional maturity help you to see,
While my heart finds comfort in healing legacy.

Like the rising sun,
The mystic's path calls, blazing,
Transcending sin's hell.

A Mystic's Path

In the darkness of the night, I seek a path,
To find a way to connect and laugh,
With the divine that lies within my heart,
And find a route to make a brand-new start.

Organized religion was never my thing,
But still, I long to find my magical wings,
Of the mystical truths that still remain,
And the light of love that will always reign.

The mystic's path is not an easy one,
But it calls to me like the rising sun,
With a promise of a deeper connection,
And a chance to find true perfection.

In this world of rules and regulations,
The mystic offers a new foundation,
A way to connect to the divine source,
And to live a life with genuine course.

For the mystic's path transcends sin, hell,
It's about love and wisdom, how to dwell,
In the heart of Source that lies within,
To live in peaceful harmony, clean.

So, let's embrace the mystic's call,
And surrender to love's great hall,
Where we find the knowing we need,
And live a pure life that's free indeed.

For the mystic's way is a path of hope,
A chance to learn the strength to cope,
With the trials of life that we all face,
And to find a way to move with grace.

Powerful thirties,
Inspiring as they unfold,
Shine bright, women true.

Ode to the Thirties

Oh, women in their thirties, how you shine,
With beauty and grace, in their vital prime.
You've weathered storms, and conquered fears,
Grown into the women you are, over the years.

Your strength and courage are inspiration,
A testament to resolute determination.
Confident, strong, and fiercely independent,
Breaking barriers and stereotypes, unrepentant.

Women in their thirties, a force to behold,
Full of experience and stories untold.
You've learned to trust your intuition,
And make decisions with conviction.

Oh, women in your thirties, how you amaze,
A true embodiment of wisdom and grace.
May you continue to shine, and inspire,
With your unwavering spirit, and inner fire.

Contrition spirals,
Family protector, consumed,
Martyrdom assumed.

The Martyr

In parenthood, I took an oath to protect,
But guilt and shame soon entered the fray,
My inner demons, I had to intercept.

I shielded my children, with fear that wrecked,
A toxic cycle, I could no longer delay,
In parenthood, I took an oath to protect.

Scarcity of safety, I could not deflect,
Control became my weapon, day by day,
My inner demons, I had to intercept.

The insecurities, I wouldn't misdirect,
Transferred with ease, to those dearer,
In parenthood, I took an oath to protect.

My children's essence, I had to reflect,
A light that shone bright, in every way,
My inner demons, I had to intercept.

I broke the cycle, and learned to connect,
With my children's true selves, every day,
In parenthood, I took an oath to protect,
My inner demons, I had to intercept.

Ships pass in the night,
Fleeting dream, the end it seems,
But a common theme.

Fleeting Dream

Two sonnets pass like ships in the night,
Each with a story, each with a plight,
One seeking love, the other its destiny,
Their courses set, their fates no mystery.

The first sonnet tells of a love so pure,
Two souls entwined, forever to endure,
Their passion burning bright, like a star,
Guiding them through life, near and far.

But alas, their paths were not to meet,
Two ships passing, barely to greet,
Their love but a moment, a flicker in time,
A memory cherished but left behind.

The second sonnet speaks of a different fate,
Of a ship tossed by waves, a turbulent state,
Its course uncertain, its destiny unclear,
But still, it sails on, in the face of fear.

Two ships passing, each with a story to tell,
One of love, the other of a turbulent swell,
But in the end, they share a common theme,
Of ships passing in the night, a fleeting dream.

Once like a robot,
Following rules, a captive,
Soul lost, spirit caged.

On Autopilot

Amidst a world of order and control,
I once was like a robot, following rules.
My mind was captive, trapped in a role,
Obedient, I was just one of many tools.

I marched along, my thoughts on autopilot,
Blind to the shadows and the truth they hid.
My soul was lost, my spirit not quite,
As if a prisoner in a closed pyramid.

But then a spark, a moment in time,
A catalyst for change, a shift in my being.
I found my voice, I let my heart shine,
A new chapter, a beginning worth seeing.

No longer bound by conformity's sway,
My soul is free, and I lead my own way.

Phobia's control,
Overbearing starring role,
Self-reliance toll.

Helicopter Mom

As a parent of little ones, I held them tight,
A helicopter mom, hovering day, and night,
To protect them from all of life's scary harms,
And ensure their happiness with my loving arms.

My fear drove me to take control of their ways,
To manage their world with my overbearing gaze,
As they grew, my momism suffocated their dare,
My actions delayed their capacity to be aware.

But with bravery, I learned to let go of their hands,
To witness their strength and courage to make plans,
To see their growth, a joyous sight to behold,
As they embrace life with all their might and mold.

I no longer hover and dictate their path,
But guide them with love, let them do the math,
Encouraging them to explore and discover,
To learn from failures and boldly recover.

For in giving them independence and space,
We nurture their confidence and inner grace,
And in doing so, we allow them to fly,
To find their own way, under the vast blue sky.

Weight of sorrow's press,
Chains upon my heart, no less.
World grey, colorless.

Weight of Sorrow

In the depths of my misery,
Where darkness reigns supreme,
The soul is crushed and weary,
And hope is but a dream.

The weight of sorrow presses down,
Like chains upon my heart,
And all the world is grey and brown,
No color to impart.

The tears flow freely day and night,
As pain consumes my soul,
And all that's left is bitter blight,
As misery takes its nasty toll.

But in the midst of all this pain,
A spark of light may shine,
And in that glimmer, hope remains,
The hope that's pure and mine.

For in the depths of misery,
We find a strength within,
To rise above our history,
And start anew again.

So let the tears flow as they may,
And let the pain be felt,
For in the end, we'll find a way,
To dissolve the hurt and melt.

The misery that we once knew,
Will fade into the past,
And we'll emerge anew,
Stronger than we were last.

Bitter words wound,
Silent response when attuned.
Fear and anger hound.

Bitter Words

Oh, the power of words, how they wound,
When triggered, giving silence in response,
A spiral of aching and hurt was attuned,
My angst and anger, unkind ensconce.

But now, I see the harm my silence wrought,
The sadness I caused my child, does ache,
With bitter words, our love was soon untaught,
And my own hurt was all that I could take.

So, I vow to break this cycle of pain,
And heal the wounds dwell deep within,
To choose my words with care, love's refrain,
And let my heart be filled with calm to win.

Oh, the power of words, how they can heal,
When spoken from a place of love so real,
With kindness, empathy, and gentle feel,
Our love will reign and forever seal.

So, I'll listen to my child's heart so pure,
And validate their feelings with my love,
Our bond will be strong, of this I am sure,
And together, we'll rise to the stars above.

Superwoman, stop,
Take off the cape, find escape,
Don't forget to rest.

Superwoman Complex

*She carries the world on her shoulders,
A superwoman, invincible and bolder.
With a heart full of good, a mind so strong,
She tackles each challenge, all day long.*

*In her forties, she never stops, never slows,
A superwoman, always on the go.
But beneath the mask, the cape she wears,
Is a human heart, with fears and cares.*

*Her juggling powers, a blessing and curse,
As she strives for perfection, and nothing less.
In her quest for excellence, she forgets to rest,
And loses sight of what makes her blessed.*

*Oh superwoman, take off your cape,
And let your human heart, find its escape.
You don't have to be perfect, or do it all,
Just be true to yourself and answer your call.*

*For in your vulnerability, rests your strength,
And in your imperfection, your beauty at length.
So, embrace your flaws, let go of the complex,
And remember, even superwomen need a rest.*

Tiny hands and feet,
Reflect our actions, our trust,
They are precious art.

Precious Art

We shape the future of our young,
Their eyes, a mirror of our every move,
Our actions, like a song that they have sung,
With every step, we have a chance to improve.

But we must not let them fall to technology's lure,
For screens and devices cannot replace,
The magic of nature, a love that is pure,
And the beauty of life, found in every face.

We must be the tutors, lead by example,
Teach them the value of hard work and love,
And guide them to their hearts, so ample,
Let them shine, like sparkly stars up above.

For in their hands rests the future, bright,
A world that needs their unique light.

Passive aggression,
Words like knives, hidden anger,
Disguise falls away.

Speaking Direct

I say one thing, but mean another,
A sly remark, a delicate poke,
My words a cover for the anger,
That I can't bring myself to stoke.

Passive aggression is my game,
A way to vent without the blame,
To keep my anger hidden, tamed,
And avoid conflict without shame.

But you see through my subtle jabs,
The way I bend the words like knives,
I cannot hide the fury from your grabs,
No matter how much I try to disguise.

So, now I speak my truth, direct and clear,
For my passiveness only breeds the fear,
And though it may seem easy, my dear,
It's tough unravelling my love's cheer.

Children reflect us,
Values, actions, and habits,
Guide them with great care.

They Mirror

Children just mirror our actions,
Our values, and our distractions,
Let's guide them towards a brighter light,
Empower their voice and their inner might.

We must lead by example and show them love,
To teach them kindness and empathy, plenty of,
Respecting nature and all living beings,
Letting go of fake materialistic things.

Let's nurture their novelty and imagination,
And not stifle their creativity with limitations,
Let them explore and learn in their own way,
And watch them blossom each and every day.

For they are the future, the hope of our land,
And it's up to us to help them understand,
That they are unique and worthy of love,
And they can make a difference, rise above.

So, let's lead with grace and compassion,
And help them see their own inner passion,
Let's guide them towards a better tomorrow,
And let them lead and flourish, without sorrow.

Children just mirror our actions,
Our values, and our distractions,
Let's guide them towards a brighter light,
Empower their voice and their inner might.

Karmic trauma's hold,
Heart heavy with pain and woe,
Aching, bleeding soul.

Karmic Broth

*In the karmic broth of trauma,
I once found myself drowning,
Trapped in a cycle of drama,
With pain that kept compounding.*

*I blamed the world and all its ways,
For the hurt that I felt inside,
But little did I know in those days,
It was my own wounds I had to abide.*

*My heart was aching and bleeding,
With a pain that wouldn't subside,
And the more I tried to stop feeling,
The more I fell deeper inside.*

*I held onto a superwoman complex,
Thinking I could juggle on and on,
But soon enough, I felt perplexed,
As the weight of the world hit me strong.*

With each step, you rise
A beacon of hope and love
Guide for lost souls' path.

Uniting the Child

Sweet inner child, you once were lost,
But now you shine with strength and grace,
Your light ignites the path at any cost.

Through trials and pain, at life's frost,
You never gave up on love's embrace,
Sweet inner child, you once were lost.

In the depths of soul, you found your boss,
And let your spirit's glow set the pace,
Your light ignites the path at any cost.

You rise higher, a mystic embossed,
A beacon of hope in life's race,
Sweet inner child, you once were lost.

With peace as your guide, never exhaust,
Championing others with divine grace,
Your light ignites the path at any cost.

Amidst the darkness,
Her heart was a shining light,
Safe in her refuge.

Vital Lesson

Becoming a parent is quite the task,
There's no guidebook or simple ask,
No instructions for how to raise,
Or how to navigate life's maze.

Mistakes will come, that's for sure,
And when they do, it can feel a blur,
Remorse and guilt may fill your mind,
But don't forget, forgiveness you find.

Our kids don't mend our pain,
Or to be our therapist, to explain,
We take responsibility for what we do,
And let them just be children, too.

I'm mindful of my energy and vibes,
And how they can affect their little lives,
Listening without judgment is key,
To creating a space where they feel free.

Encourage their creativity and their dreams,
And celebrate their uniqueness, so it seems,
Praise their efforts, not just success,
And teach them to enjoy life's process.

Parenting is a journey, never done,
But with patience, kindness, and a little fun,
We'll grow and learn every single day,
And be the best role model, come what may.

Illness, trauma's bold,
Flashbacks, numbness taking hold,
Darkness, distrust bold.

Chronic Illness

*With life's curveball thrown at me,
My soul was tested heavily.
My sister's near-death was the start,
Of a journey that strained my heart.*

*I struggled to self-regulate,
As I faced this heavy weight.
Choices made were not the best,
A cry for help, a failed test.*

*My body went into freeze response,
Playing dead, trying to cope.
Running was no longer an option,
Vexing became my concoction.*

*This threat resulted in illness,
Trauma, flashbacks, no stillness.
I felt disoriented and numb,
No strength to overcome.*

*Withdrawing from the game,
Viewing life with pessimistic aim.
Depression took hold of me, again,
My body's way of response, a bane.*

*But within me lay a desire,
To rise from this gloomy mire.
To take control and master,
To emerge from the disaster.*

*I slowly found my way,
To heal and face another day.
My soul now stronger and braver,
As I rose from the ashes, a self-master.*

Wake-up call, so clear,
Lifeline needed, spirit near,
Grateful, no more fear.

A Wake-Up Call

*On the path to heal,
my body and soul,
my pain had developed,
beyond control.*

*More than physical,
the high pitch sounds,
stemmed from my core
emotional wounds.*

*I had lost my way
in probing thought,
steering into a brick wall,
I stopped and fought.*

*It was a wakeup call,
this lifeline was needed,
My spirit guided,
grateful it interceded.*

Writing to expose,
Childhood shadows, tear-stained woes,
Truth spoken, power rose.

Heart of a Warrior

*I began writing,
exposing the shadows,
Tear-stained pages soaked
by childhood wallows.*

*I reclaimed my power
and spoke my truth,
Heart of a warrior,
ailments of youth.*

*This fictional story,
Was infused by events,
Of past unhealed worry,
That echoed my parents.*

*It took great courage
to unveil the secrets,
The doubt and fear
filled me with regrets.*

*But my healing required
radical responsibility,
to realize that the past
didn't dictate my ability.*

*I freed my soul,
connecting with divine,
Awakened and lit,
letting my grace shine.*

Persistent whispers,
Insecure thoughts, mind's blisters,
Stealing joy, denied.

Insecure Thoughts

Oh, insecure thoughts, how you do persist,
Your nagging whispers that I cannot resist.
You cloud my mind, you steal my joy away,
You tell me I am not enough today.

You point out every flaw, every mistake,
You amplify my doubts and make me shake.
You keep me up at night with worried fears,
You undermine my confidence and smear.

But still, I cannot help but recognize,
That you are a part of me, in disguise.
You stem from pain and trauma I have felt,
From wounds I thought I had long ago dealt.

Even when you bring me down at times,
I will try to understand your rhymes.
Listening to what you have to say,
And show you love and kindness every day.

For maybe then, you'll start to lose your hold,
And I'll find peace, and courage to be bold.
So, insecure feelings, though you be a pest,
I'll face you head-on and put you to rest.

Burden etched, bloodstream,
Woman's worth less, a man's dream,
Prove value, redeem.

The Burn Out

I juggled life attached to my superwoman,
Work, family, home, MBA, just as worthy as man.
I drove myself beyond my physical limits,
Over scheduling my kids masking my gimmicks.

This burden was etched into my bloodstream,
A woman wasn't as worthy as a man's dream.
Constantly proving my value to gain respect,
I projected my lack, suffering, and neglect.

It was a call to action from my spirit, a séance,
I had to heal the pain of ancestral cycle of chaos.
My grandparents emerged from domestic violence,
An epoch of famine, prejudice, abuse of substance.

My parents were raised with false expectations,
repressed emotions, alcohol misuse, toxic relations.
Their co-dependency and untreated mental illness,
Fueled their unregulated feelings with sadness.

No wonder my generation holds these imprints,
With their people pleasing manners, DNA hints.
Depression, anxiety, burn-out, and struggle,
Were my innate emotive deficits to juggle.

After eighteen months, physical constraint,
My well ran dry, no energy left to give in this saint.
Disempowered, sapped of precious resource,
Neglecting my health, I drained my life force.

The stress induced mental and physical fatigue,
collapsing my nervous system, out of my league.
After a week in my bed, unable to move,
I lost twenty pounds, too weak to find my groove.

Power within, soul,
Heal the wounds, make spirit strong,
Journey to the light.

Power Within

Deep within thy soul, lies dormant power,
That guides thee to reach thy destined goal,
Mending the wounds that cause thy heart to cower,
Bolstering thy spirit to make thee whole.

Each moment, a precious gift to cherish,
To love and nurture thyself with great care,
For thou art worthy of all that will flourish,
In thy life, with grace and love to spare.

Let thy spirit rise and shine with great flare,
With strength and hope, let thy heart take flight,
For in the midst of turmoil, thou shalt dare,
To conquer all, with thy will to ignite.

Through trials and hardships, thou shalt prevail,
With courage and devotion, thou shalt never fail.

Forgiveness takes time,
A personal journey's pace,
Confusion dissolves.

Raw Emotions

From a troubled state, my path did begin,
Old cycles and rejection's sting within,
My heart in pain, seeking healing's balm,
Energy fields in need of soothing calm.

Boundaries crossed, anger and grief arise,
Natural response to violation, wise,
Raw emotions, experiences to face,
Forgiveness, a personal journey's pace.

Society teaches to repress emotions,
Meet expectations, suppress pain notions,
But in doing so, our hearts feel broken,
Tolerant family, words left unspoken.

To clear dark coding and karmic ties,
I unified my being, purified my soul's eyes,
Releasing self-sabotage and ego's chains,
Feminine wounds healed, no more pains.

Underlying fears emerged, uncertainty,
Disorientation, but rebirth brought clarity,
Inner stillness emerged, dread melted away,
And joy and love's elation is here to stay.

Confusion dissolved, clarity in sight,
A higher timeline's paradigm, now in flight,
Balanced and aligned, walking the pathway,
Sacred light's freedom codes, in my soul to stay.

Two wolves in our soul,
One of shadow, one of light,
Battle for control.

Proverb of Wolves

There's a battle inside every soul,
Two wolves that are vying for control,
The shadow one's anger and greed,
Jealousy and ego, indeed,
While the light's sympathy, is the whole.

The light wolf's pure, humble, and kind,
Empathetic, truthful, peace aligned,
With deception and all its kin,
Love and compassion always win,
In this daily battle of the mind.

It's up to us to choose who wins,
Which wolf inside takes the reins,
Feed the light one, it will grow,
And its beam will always glow,
For in this fight, the victor gains.

Full circle my tale,
From depths of ache to the light,
Heart complete with might.

Recycling Doubt

A realization came, I must break free,
From cycles that had held me down so tight,
To confront the pain and doubts that I see,
And let my spirit soar with newfound might.

I faced my inner critic with great care,
Found strength in my self-belief and grace,
Honoring myself with love beyond compare,
Accepting my path with an open embrace.

Now I aim to live in a higher realm of light,
With joy, peace, and a newfound sensation,
I am the creator of my own spirit's delight,
Free from cycles of toxicity and degradation.

My story comes full circle, a journey of the soul,
From depths of anguish to the beauty of divine,
With a heart full of love, my essence whole,
Hugging my own inner power, I shine.

Courage starts with truth,
Transforms darkness into light,
Soul's purpose blossoms.

Getting Real

It's vital to admit that I exist for a reason,
A crucial step towards my worthiness,
Treating myself with dignity and vision,
Unlocks my inner discernment's finesse.

My deepest source of strength is devotion,
A memory of my first step to liberation,
Yet, voices push me down a rabbit hole,
Of neurotic spirals and dark fabrication.

I sought a somatic therapist to release my stress,
Acknowledging my feelings with self-care,
The findings expose a disability to address,
OCD, depression, and anxiety, I couldn't bear.

The first step towards courage was getting real,
To label my struggles without negative chatter,
Accepting that there's something more to reveal,
Joy's first step lies in my human avatar's nature.

With newfound self-awareness, I can grow,
Transforming darkness into light and blossom,
The first step towards progress is mine to show,
My soul's purpose shining brightly in its bosom.

Surrender holds key,
Freedom, joy, and flow of life,
Worries start to cease.

Expectations

*In days of old, the bards would sing
Of knights and ladies fair,
But here's a tale of a different thing,
Of expectations that we bear.*

*We hold on tight to what we know,
To what we think is right,
But in our grasp, we lose the glow,
Of the present's precious light.*

*The image in our minds we craft,
Becomes a cage we're in,
And as we focus on what's lacked,
We lose the chance to win.*

*To truly live, we must let go,
Of control and our desire,
And trust in what we do not know,
Let our hearts become a pyre.*

*For in surrender, we find the key,
To freedom, joy, and peace,
And in the flow of life's great sea,
Our worries start to cease.*

*So let go of expectations bold,
And trust the universe's sway,
For in the present's beauty untold,
Remains our happiness each day.*

Trials bring lessons new,
Resilience won't crumble,
Standing by their side.

Loving Care

With tender care, I raised my precious young,
Nurturing them with all my heart and soul,
Instilling in their minds that they are strong,
And teaching them to be their own control.

Through trial and error, we would stumble,
And with each fall, we learned a lesson new,
Their resilience would grow and never crumble,
As I stood by their side, they always knew.

With open hearts and minds, we did engage,
Connecting safely with no shame or fear,
Their voices heard, they did not feel caged,
Their spirits lifted, their path was clear.

They have grown and flown the nest away,
But in my heart, their memories remain,
As I reflect on the love shared each day,
Grateful for the joy and sunbeams they sustain.

Courage to seek help,
Self-understanding to rise,
Precious path above.

Acknowledging Triggers

With guidance from therapy, I learned to see,
The triggers that could send me in a spin,
I learned to care for myself when in need.

Setting boundaries, speaking up for me,
Most challenging tasks for me to begin,
But with guidance, I learned to see.

Celebrating my gifts and my unique degree,
I found my voice and let it softly ring,
And I learned to care for myself when in need.

Through my healing journey, truth did decree,
Community offers a helping hand to prevail,
With guidance, I learned to see.

Resilience and proof from others, did feed,
My worthiness that lay deep within,
I learned to care for myself when in need.

Courage led me to seek self-love, to be,
A path precious to rise above the din,
With guidance, I learned to see,
I learned to care for myself when in need.

Soft twigs carefully placed,
Young ones soon to wear a crown,
Nature's miracle.

Robin's Flight

The robins have flown back in town,
In the trees, they chirp up and down,
They build their warm nests,
With soft twigs, they invest,
And their young ones will soon wear a crown.

Raise voices up high,
Join in song with joyful cry,
Love in melody.

Permission to Feel

Oh, voice of mine, how brave and true,
You broke the silence, and broke through,
The pain and fear that held you down,
Permission to feel with a resounding sound.

Oh, how you sang of hope and light,
Of healing and taking charge all right,
And in your words, we all could see,
A path to freedom and victory.

With every note, you soared above,
And showed us all the power of love,
The capacity to heal and forgive,
To rise again, and truly live.

Oh, voice of mine, how strong and clear,
You touched our hearts, and eased our fear,
And in your courage, we all could find,
The strength to leave our past behind.

So let us raise our voices high,
And join in song with a joyful cry,
For with your voice, we all can see,
The beauty of our own melody.

Time to cleanse, release,
Old wounds, blockages, find peace,
Face patterns, let go.

Spring Cleaning

In the depths of my soul, I felt the need,
To wash away the dirt and debris,
From all the people-pleasing ways,
That led to fragmentation and disarray.

I knew it was time to cleanse and release,
Old wounds and blockages, to find peace,
To face the patterns of my past,
And let go of the pain that couldn't last.

Duplicity left me lacking trust,
Feeling undervalued, I must,
Find a way to move past the hurt,
And allow my heart to open, assert.

By focusing my attention and awareness,
I cracked my star gate, found the fairness,
That had been missing from my life,
And revealed a portal of truth that was rife.

With magic, treasures, and wisdom to behold,
Blessings from heaven and a source so bold,
That shifted my consciousness to a higher state,
And allowed me to receive love, that's my fate.

So now I stand here, a soul renewed,
Washed clean from the pain of my old view,
Ready to embrace the blessings of this life,
And face each day with courage, without strife.

Amidst the chaos,
Stillness can be found within,
Letting go with grace.

Emotional Currents

Emotional currents, how strong they flow,
Like ocean waves that crash upon the shore,
And just like tides that rise and then plateau,
These feelings can sweep us up and then more.

They come in swells, in moments high and low,
A force that seems beyond our mortal wit,
But even though we feel like we must go,
These waves will recede, and calm will begin.

Take a moment to heal and release the past,
Breathe in the air and exhale in a blast.
For the ocean and human form are divine,
Stay centered and aligned, let your light shine.

When emotional waves come crashing down,
Stay strong and soon quiet will be found.
For just like the sea, you will weather the storm,
And find your way back to life transformed.

For just like oceans, our emotions shift,
From calm to rough, from storm to breeze,
And though they seem to take an endless drift,
These currents will subside, and we'll find ease.

So let us not resist, but learn to ride,
These tides of life, with grace and peace inside.

Visual focus,
Where surrender finds release,
Worries start to cease.

Becoming the Witness

Visual centering, a technique so divine,
A way to calm my fears and ease my mind,
With each breath, I witness my inner state,
And find peace within, present moment's gate.

My focus moves from external to internal,
As I center my awareness and become the kernel,
Of my being, the seat of my consciousness,
A place of stillness, free from all turbulence.

In this state of surrender, I find release,
And all my worries begin to cease,
I open up to receive divine guidance,
And my intuition awakens with vibrance.

My stress and anxiety dissolve away,
As I enter a state of relaxation, each day,
And with clarity of thought, my cognition sharpens,
Unlocking dormant powers, my potential deepens.

Visual centering, a technique so grand,
A tool for my inner journey, a helping hand,
Guiding me to self-regulate and find my flow,
In the alignment of life, where I can truly grow.

Blossoming anew,
I released my past burden,
Heart now unshackled.

Identity Unmasked

Honoring the vision of how I want to feel,
I peeled off the layers of the past's ordeal,
Embracing the essence of self-reveal.

Guided by counseling's guiding wheel,
I learned to let go of drama and heal,
Honoring the vision of how I want to feel.

I unmasked my identity, courage as my seal,
And surrendered to my presence, so surreal,
Embracing the essence of self-reveal.

Confidence and security, I now feel,
As I trust the journey, life did deal,
Honoring the vision of how I want to feel.

In stillness, feeling breath of existence, so real,
Grateful for the path, with the least resistance,
Embracing the essence of self-reveal.

Day by day, I transformed my emotions to heal,
Breaking free from the past's dark ordeal,
Honoring the vision of how I want to feel,
Embracing the essence of self-reveal.

Light and dark unite,
Colors of the universe,
Beauty in contrast.

Dance of Duality

I began to realize,
the dance of duality,
Balance of my sacred,
union within was key.

I understood how I emit,
the energy of mortality,
Which clearly affected,
my views of reality.

I was trapped in cycles,
by my constant ranting,
blaming others blocked me,
from life I was wanting.

I'm here to discover,
Life's harmony to shine,
The polarized music,
strokes of the divine.

Together we grew,
In a bond of love and trust,
Strong family base.

Fostering Sovereignty

With my best ability, I nurtured my children,
Fostering sovereignty, giving them freedom,
Mistakes were made, lessons were learned,
Building resilience, with trust unconcerned.

Open communication, free from judgement,
Allowed safe expression, without adjustment,
Honoring and respecting, their unique path,
Tweaking my emotions, without any wrath.

Being present, I show pure intention,
Listening to their needs, transformation,
Praising creativity, in their self-expression,
Empowering their growth, no reservation.

With love and care, I nurtured their being,
Fostering their potential, with no ceiling,
Guiding their journey, with grace's foresight,
Trusting their process, with love as my light.

Thoughts once insecure,
Whispered doubts, uncertainty,
Challenged and transformed.

The Nagging

*There once were some thoughts insecure,
That made me feel sad and unsure,
They whispered and nagged,
My confidence sagged,
But I faced them and found a cure.*

Love of self not greed,
Key to a life humane, kind,
Everlasting flame.

Love of Self

Amidst the chaos of life's daily grind,
It's easy to forget oneself and strife,
To seek approval of others, and to find,
Self-worth and meaning in others' life.

Yet deep within, lies a sacred space,
A haven of love, and an endless grace,
A place where we can seek and find,
The light of self-love, pure and divine.

Love of self is not selfishness, as some say,
It's a commitment to honor and cherish,
Our own being, and our unique way,
To embrace ourselves, and never perish.

So let us love ourselves, and never wane,
For self-love is the key to a life humane.

Divine spark within,
Heart portal activated,
Burning fake layers.

White Beams

In my third decade, the light emerged,
Switched on my pineal, white beams surged.
I practiced ancient lore, cleansing with codes,
Unlocking the 72 names of Divine in loads.

I learned that childhood trauma impacted,
All types of bloodlines, wounds that persisted.
These painful experiences of abuse,
Etched by a series of gloom and blues.

I was not unique or alone in my misery,
The slaughter of tribes fueled my enquiry.
Survivors of our native holocaust,
Ignited the truth with tears to exhaust.

Together, we lived in unconsciousness,
Building walls and masks to handle the mess.
I had to heal my codependent wounding,
This clarity triggered disgrace by conceding.

I tapped into my multidimensional essence,
decoding the language of existence.
Walking through the flame of self-discovery,
Burning away the fake layers with slow recovery.

I witnessed the divine spark in all as I mature,
My heart portal activated by their true nature.
Becoming mindful of the effects of my words,
Observing my deeds laced by silver cords.

Tender beam of light,
Her gaze makes the soul glow bright,
In daughter's eyes found.

My Daughter's Eyes

In my daughter's eyes, I see
A realm that's filled with possibility
A home where love and hope abound
And joy and wonder always surround.

Each time I gaze upon her face
I feel my heart start to race
For in her eyes, I find a light
That shines so pure and so bright.

Her eyes, like precious jewels gleam
With such a warm and tender beam
And when she looks at me just so
I feel my soul begin to glow.

In those deep and wondrous eyes
I see a future of equality and rise
A world of promise, of endless wisdom
Where everything flows in her Queendom.

Oh, how I cherish my daughter's eyes
For her soul is magic that defies
All the worries, anxiety, and pain
She brings me back to life again.

So, here's to all our daughter's debut
May they always shine like morning dew
And light their path with abundance to go
Through all life's ups and downs, high and low.

Wounded inner child,
Virtue in her shining heart,
Deserving pleasure.

Knowing my Worth

My inner child once lived in dread and pain,
With wounds that left her feeling small and frail,
But now she stands with worth and light again.

No longer seeking validation in vain,
Or hiding in the shadows of betrayal,
My inner child once lived in dread and pain.

With courage and compassion, she'll remain,
I will never let her spirit be derailed,
For now, she stands with worth and light again.

She knows her value, not held in chains,
No longer trapped in hurt that once prevailed,
My inner child once lived in dread and pain.

With kindness, she's come to ascertain,
And her true identity cannot be curtailed,
For now, she stands with worth and light again.

Embracing all that's good, she'll not refrain,
From living life in ways that won't impale,
My inner child once lived in dread and pain,
But now she stands with worth and light again.

Alchemy at work,
Breaking spells with lion's perks,
Claws sharpened to win.

Breaker of Spells

I cocooned in silence, I won't deny
This radiant transformed butterfly
Now I roar in the ethers
A fierce warrior of creatures.

I cannot be controlled, I decree
My waters are pure and run free
I erupt the corrupt and deviant dams
With a sacred current, the wrath that jams.

I am an alchemist, a breaker of spells
Of sinful black magic that certainly sells
I have alerted the lionesses within
Sharpening claws, much to their chagrin.

In a world that's filled with chaos and strife
We are the one who brings balance to life
With a steady hand and a gentle touch
We protect the young from harm and such.

For in the eyes of a child, there is a spark
A flame that blazes, even in the dark
It is our duty to maintain it aflame
And shield it from the forces of shame.

We are the protectors of all that is right
A beacon of hope, a guiding light
In our presence, all fears disappear
And the innocent can laugh without a tear.

Oh, advocates of purity, let's sing your praise
For you light up our world with caring ways
May you always shine like the brightest star
And guide us all to a world that is free from scars.

Focus on my soul,
Commitment to peace alone,
Heart's powerful guide.

Focus of Energy

When I stopped fretting about other thoughts,
And focused on my soul's intent sought,
My energy levels rose and soared,
With things that brought me bliss and more.

I realized that this journey is mine,
The most crucial commitment to divine,
Accepting divergent qualities with pride,
I open my heart's intensity to guide.

Life became more fulfilling, taking back my power,
Replaced people pleasing with self-finding by hour,
No more endless patterns of worry and sorrow,
Only my growth and co-creation to follow.

Each fear and anxiety leaked my energy,
Fueling resistance and stagnation, I see,
But now I choose to focus on expansion,
And honor the rareness of my own creation.

So let my heart's truest intentions guide,
As I walk my path with purpose and stride,
Embracing my rare qualities and ways,
Living my life with joy and grace, I pray.

Entwined, we cling tight,
Co-dependency's embrace,
Lost in dance's plight.

Co-dependency

In co-dependency we find ourselves lost,
Entwined in a dance we can't escape,
Our lives so tangled at a great cost,
We cling to one another with no shape.

We live in fear of staying alone,
Afraid to let go and find our own way,
Our roots so tangled that we can't atone,
To separate from this entangled display.

But in this cycle, we forget our worth,
And ignore our own desires and needs,
Our love comes from a place of dearth,
And only feeds the cycle that it breeds.

Let us break free from this unhealthy tie,
And find the beauty in our own light to fly.

Piercing dark with light,
Courageous heart leads the way,
With purpose, we shine.

Piercing the Darkness

Amidst the turmoil, I stand tall and strong,
My voice a beacon, a call to belong.
A spirit unbroken, my will unyielding,
I speak for the silenced, pain revealing.

I am the light that pierces the darkness,
The hope that ignites, a fire to harness.
With courage as my guide, I forge ahead,
Fueled by the love that my heart has fed.

No more will I cower, no more will I hide,
I step in my power, my truth amplified.
With each move I make, I leave fear behind,
My soul alight, my purpose defined.

For the battle may rage, and the night is long,
But I know that I belong, I know I am strong.
And in the face of adversity, I will rise,
A warrior of love, with unwavering eyes.

Diverse minds and hearts,
Weaving the tapestry art,
Honoring each part.

Divergent Minds

Let's celebrate neurodiversity,
Embrace the beauty and strength,
Breaking down barriers with clarity,
And create a world of equal length.

With empathy and understanding,
We can foster a globe of true diversity,
Where all can thrive, souls expanding,
And feel accepted, with no adversity.

Oh, neurodiversity, how we adore,
Unique perspectives, that we implore,
With love and support, we open the door,
To a world of inclusion, forevermore.

Let's unite with loving hearts and support,
And make the world a better place for all,
Honoring neurodiversity, and its full import,
Creating a realm where we can stand tall.

Amidst the chaos,
Inside my heart, peace I find,
Solace and stillness.

Solace and Stillness

Inside my heart, I find peace of mind,
Away from the chaos and the blinding sight,
The place where solace and stillness I can find.

The noise and chatter, I leave them behind,
To listen to the whispers of stars at night,
Inside my heart, I find peace of mind.

The starlight glows so gentle and kind,
A sight that fills my soul with pure delight,
The place where solace and stillness I can find.

In this moment, my troubles are confined,
The worries of the day fade out of sight,
Inside my heart, I find peace of mind.

The world slows down, it becomes less unkind,
And everything feels okay, just for tonight,
The place where solace and stillness I can find.

With every breath, I leave my cares behind,
In this haven, I feel a sense of flight,
Inside my heart, I find peace of mind,
The place where solace and stillness I can find.

Fourth Decade: Shifting into Purpose

Canvas on the stand
Brush strokes bring the scene to life
Easel holds the dream

Warriors' strength stirs,
My awakening begins,
Activation born.

Becoming Aware

My activation is a story to behold,
Triggered by warriors, an occupation foretold.
Their brave resilience shed light on my suffering,
Awakening to my truth required some buffering.

I had long enabled the chaos to reign,
But now a new self-awareness to gain.
The journey ahead, both winding and steep,
A quest to unravel and discover the deep.

It was a gradual process of realization,
To accept my identity, my soul's foundation.
And in the face of my insight's temptation,
I took responsibility, a mindful dedication.

The shattering of illusions, a tumultuous storm,
Yet my spirit persisted, steadfast and strong.
The journey homeward, a challenging task,
But to be free, I shed the weight of the past.

The initiation begins, my story unfolds,
I am transforming, a new life to behold.

Love's pure magic spell,
Emotion and fabric sewn,
Mystery in all.

Magic of Love

Love is pure magic,
A state of being,
Not born of tragic.
It flows in the air,
Not just emotion,
Sewn with fabric flair.
It's in all living things,
A mystery of stars,
Found on cosmic wings.
Love works in such ways,
Both magnificent,
And strange, it's ablaze.
There's nothing in life,
Love cannot change,
If we let go strife.
It can lift mountains,
And transform oceans,
With rhythms of fountains.
The most common seed,
Changes with splendor,
Even the normal weed.
Love is unselfish,
Pure, gentle, and kind,
That isn't jealous.
It's the essence,
Of the sacred divine,
Flowing with presence.
Love is the answer,
We are all seeking,
In semantic dancers.
Love can't be bought,
It's priceless, no measure,
Love is magic, not taught,
In life's golden treasure.

Hidden realms unfold,
Insights bring self-awareness,
Wisdom expands soul.

A Lifelong Path

Oh, sweet freedom born of love's choice,
Breaking chains of self-sabotage with joyous voice,
Once lost, now found, consciousness came alive,
Releasing me from zombie state, emotions revive.

Awareness of hidden realms of life beyond,
Bringing incredible insights of which I'm fond,
With new information to integrate and learn,
A chance for self-actualization to yearn.

Even with intuition, there are still attachments,
Journey of healing is a lifelong path, detachment,
But applying wisdom with clarity in hand,
Expands the soul, into the mystery we expand.

I step into the unknown celestial wave,
With pure love and awareness, my only crave,
Liberating me from conditioned things,
Flying high with my newfound wings.

Beneath starry sky,
A tranquil evening goes by,
Hush we can't deny.

The Observer

Awakened soul, your story is grand,
From a state of slumber, you rose with a stand,
Separated from your higher self, feeling lost,
But you kept going, no matter the cost.

You ventured out, seeking to enforce,
Your quest for truth, you felt no remorse,
With premonitions, you linked to Source,
The signs of intervention, you didn't ignore.

You followed symbols, in nature and in art,
Numerology and geometry, with angelic heart,
Challenging life, holding space for your own,
You unveiled the hidden truths, unknown.

Your identity unraveled, a mask no more,
A world of energy, you began to explore,
Aligning with frequencies of pure synergy,
Becoming the observer, not the false entity.

Lessons learned, trials and pain endured,
A catalyst that awakens souls, for sure,
Now you stand tall, radiant, and bold,
Your spirit rekindled, a story to be told.

Kindness, compassion,
Ripple out like pebbles tossed,
Spreading love beyond.

Karmic Points

My inner wisdom speaks of Karma's force,
A power that transcends, a cosmic course.
Good or bad, it comes back around,
A cycle of cause and effect, abound.

Good Karma is born of heartfelt intention,
Of kindness, compassion, and attention.
It ripples out like a pebble in a pond,
Touching hearts, spreading love beyond.

Bad Karma is amassed from shadow side,
A reflection of our bruised ego's pride.
Deceit, manipulation, and attachment,
Bring negative energy and detachment.

To accrue good Karma, we must be true,
Honest, real, and humble in all we do.
It's not about reward or recognition,
But living with grace and pure intention.

So let us live in harmony and peace,
And let our positive Karma increase.
Let love be the driving force within,
Allow our good deeds to vibrate and win.

Two forces at play,
Opposite, yet both needed,
Life in balance sway.

Force of Balance

Polarity, the force that gives us balance,
A cosmic dance, equal and opposite stance,
Creating a world complex and refined.

Your positive and negative charges, intertwined,
Bear the essence of our universe's expanse,
Polarity, the force that gives us balance.

In this waltz of space, formed objects we find,
A spectacle of contrast, its grandeur enhanced,
Creating a world complex and refined.

Without your duality, life would be confined,
Devoid of vitality, existence of chance,
Polarity, the force that gives us balance.

We're blessed with your universal design,
A spectacle of wonder of abundance,
For polarity, you're the core of our domain.

So let us embrace your force, divine,
And revel in the magic of your cosmic dance,
Polarity, the force that gives us balance,
Creating a world complex and refined.

Shedding the old skin,
Agony released, fly free,
Instincts guide my quest.

Letting Go

With instincts as my guide, I went on a quest,
To shed my skin and become anew,
My mystical journey put me to the test.

Forgiving those who hurt me, I found rest,
Letting go all agony, my freedom to pursue,
With instincts as my guide, I went on a quest.

Lessons learning, I transform with strength,
No longer a pleaser, but a warrior light,
My mystical journey put me to the test.

My reality clear, with peace abreast,
Probing science, seeking an inner truth,
With instincts as my guide, I went on a quest

Pursuing the I AM, my soul would pervade,
Integrating and clearing, vision so new,
My mystical journey put me to the test.

United with pure spirit, my path is blessed,
Each step I take, I rise with wisdom,
With instincts as my guide, I went on a quest,
My mystical journey put me to the test.

The wounds of the heart
Are eased by forgiveness' balm,
Soul finds healing.

Fortitude to Forgive

Oh, forgiveness, how great thou art,
A balm for the wounded heart,
A salve that heals the deepest pain,
And brings us peace and love again.

Through trials and tribulations, we endure,
Our souls fractured, the ego's impure,
But forgiveness is a path we can take,
To release the pain, to let go of the ache.

It takes fortitude to forgive those who wronged,
To let go of the past and the bitterness prolonged,
But the freedom that comes with this act divine,
Brings new light, new hope, a sense of real shine.

For forgiveness is a gift we give to ourselves,
A release from suffering, a healing for our souls,
It's a choice to change the cycle of past's hold,
To rise above the hurt, to be brave and bold.

Oh, forgiveness, how great thou art,
A beacon that illuminates a fresh start,
May we embrace this gift with all our might,
And find the strength to shine with sacred light.

Achy, weary frame,
Each pain a reminder, time,
My journey to own.

Weary and Worn

My achy body, weary and worn,
Carries the weight of each passing morn.
Each ache and pain a reminder of time,
A journey that's tough, but still, it's mine.

The knots in muscles, friction in my spine,
Ribs in my back, toiled for a lifetime.
The wear and tear of daily life, whirled,
A constant battle in this physical world.

But though my body is frayed and weak,
It's a testament to the path that I seek.
Each discomfort a mark of my story,
A journey that brought me to this glory.

I've learned that my vessel is but a shell,
Housing my consciousness that truly tells.
My story of in this life and who I hope to be,
A force that can conquer any adversity.

For in this achy body, I find my strength,
The life force that conquers any length.
With depth that's strong and unrelenting,
A power enduring and never-ending.

Life's voyage unfolds,
A winding path we traverse,
Unknown destination.

Twists and Turns

In the depths of the night, when all is still,
And the moon casts shadows on windowsill,
I find myself lost in my own thoughts,
As I ponder the meaning of life's knots.

What is the purpose of this life we lead,
And what's the essence that we truly need,
To find pleasure and peace of mind,
Leaving the worries and doubts behind?

Perhaps it's in the moments of simple grace,
A smile from a loved one, a warm embrace,
Or in the beauty of the sunset's glow,
That we find the answers we seek and know.

For life is a journey, a winding road,
With twists and turns, an unpredictable code,
And though it may be hard to comprehend,
Our time on this earth will come to an end.

Let us cherish every moment we're given,
For life's a gift, we must make worth living.
In the end, it's not about what we possess,
But the love in our hearts that will truly bless.

Acupressure taps,
Meridian points unlock,
Emotional calm.

Meridian Tapping

Sometimes life is filled with turmoil,
Bringing forth my heart's despair,
Anxiety consumed me whole,
Once again, left me in disrepair.

I searched for a way to heal,
To ease the weight upon my soul,
And that's when I stumbled upon,
The magic of acupressure's toll.

Tapping on meridian points,
I felt my body come alive,
Each touch with peace and calm,
Helped me feel ease, so revived.

With every tap, my fears did expose,
And my doubts began to fade,
I found the strength to face shadows,
And let go of the mistakes I've made.

The modality brought me foresight,
A way to ease my bodily discomfort,
And regain my vitality in sight,
Finding the inner peace, I sought.

Now when anxiety comes knocking,
I know exactly what to do,
I tap away my fear and worries,
And find my strength anew.

This tapping has become my song,
The ballad of hope and renewal,
A melody of resilience and strength,
A way to conquer my inner turmoil.

Dreams astral guidance,
Symbols led to consciousness,
Demons confronted.

Resolving the Umbra

My mystical awakening was a birdsong,
An echo that revealed my right and wrong,
The truth behind the fakeness I was taught,
Since childhood, my mind was distraught.

My astral dreams, they took on many shapes,
Symbolism led me through the conscious gate,
And forced me to face the shadows deep within,
The demons that held me captive, to my chagrin.

The wounds of my inner child were the key,
The darkest corners of my psyche I did see,
Negative thoughts questioned my self-worth,
Were the barriers that kept me in the earth.

But with deep introspection, the bonds drain,
I found the multidimensional within my brain,
Resolving the umbra, embracing my true art,
I rose a phoenix, a total eclipse of the heart.

May my lessons be a clarion call for you,
Follow your heart, and find what's true,
To trust in yourself, and let your light shine,
Embracing the journey, one step at a time.

Our body speaks truth,
In whispers or painful shouts,
Listen, heal, and grow.

Vessel of Life

Our physical temple, how divine,
A foundation of life, a vessel so fine,
In perfect harmony, mind, spirit connect,
Our wisdom and destiny in alignment reflect.

With every breath, our heart beats a tune,
A natural rhythm, a symphony to consume,
For every cell, a healing energy we bring,
A daily dose of gratitude, a soulful ring.

In this awareness, our bodies we redefine,
No longer ignoring signals that we find,
But exploring the imbalances and blocks,
A journey of self-discovery, no more shocks.

Oh, emotive health, so integral and deep,
A journey to self-regulate and keep,
The particles of sentiment, so real and true,
To honor our physical state, a new hue.

Let's embrace this movement of energy,
Mind, spirit, body in perfect synergy,
In gratitude and growth, we embody our best,
Our truest self, in coherence, we're blessed.

In each story's arc,
A turning point ignites change,
Catalyst's power.

Turning Point

In every story, there's a turning point,
A moment where the plot begins to anoint,
My character had the power to change,
And become the catalyst for a new range.

She might be a hero, brave and bold,
Or an unlikely figure, with a story untold,
Someone who sees beyond the surface,
And brings new perspective with purpose.

The catalyst gives a spark of light,
And sets the stage for a new fight,
Against the darkness, against the odds,
Becoming a force that can't be stopped.

Their courage and conviction inspire,
Kindles a flame that burns brighter, higher,
A blaze that ignites the hearts of all,
And pushes them to rise and stand tall.

They might not see the fruit of their labor,
Or the seeds of change that they did savor,
But their legacy lives on, forever,
In the hearts of those with endeavor.

We honor all the catalysts of our time,
The sages who have passed, in their prime,
Let us carry on their work, with passion and might,
And become agents of change, in our own right.

Blocks of solitude,
Pathways of power arise,
Transcending limits.

Building Blocks

Molecules, building blocks of life, unseen,
Connecting my body, mind, soul, in between,
A complex network of energy and thought,
Bringing new meaning to the life I sought.

My body speaks, misaligned, it's clear,
Tension builds, a warning sign to hear,
Aches and pains, the voice of my intuition,
A call to action, a shift in position.

Emotional intelligence, a journey of growth,
Uncovering patterns, the stories they clothe,
Rewiring my mind, a path to explore,
To find my real self, my purpose, and more.

Anxiety, a weight that I often bear,
The storms of life, a burden hard to share,
But with breathwork, my mind unwinds,
A release from tension, a new outlook finds.

Constrictions born of wounds, I complain,
Blockages, patterns that I must retrain,
Finding safety in moments of play,
A tonic for my soul, a bright new day.

The particles within, a guide and a light,
To navigate through life's lows and heights,
To embrace the rhythms of my body's beat,
And find beauty in each moment I meet.

For in this solitude, my mind can soar,
And find peace in life's simple things once more,
The gentle breeze, the nightingale's song,
My soul discovers rest, where it truly belongs.

Open hearts, clear minds,
A creative spark ignites,
Limitless beauty.

Improved Creativity

In life, we must create to explore,
Our inner world, and external shore,
But sometimes trauma holds us back,
And limits our playfulness and knack.

Obligations, they can weigh us down,
And prevent us from shedding our frown,
Coping mechanisms, they can defend,
Our bodies and minds, from a bitter end.

But if we stay too long in a state,
Of constriction, it may turn to fate,
And lead to chronic illness and pain,
A life of sorrow, a life in vain.

To embody our true selves, we must,
Slowly let out the air, and trust,
That we can handle what we find,
With compassion, and gentle mind.

Scraping away the shadows, the pain,
May take time, but we'll gain,
A deeper sense of self and grace,
A lighter step, a smiling face.

Improved creativity is the key,
To connect our inner world, and see,
The beauty of our external view,
The possibilities, they're all so new.

Let's start to create, let us explore,
Let playfulness emanate from our core,
And with each step, we'll feel the light,
That shines within and guides our sight.

Playful laughter frees,
Worries drift and fade away,
Embrace life with joy.

Some Good Fun

There once was a Queen quite wise,
Who knew that play was the prize,
She laughed and she danced,
And took silly chances,
And felt her mood start to rise.

With games and silly good fun,
She felt the stress come undone,
Her mind felt renewed,
And spirit imbued,
With a joy second to none.

Let's take time for play each day,
Allowing our worries drift away,
Our mental health will improve,
As we laugh, dance, and groove,
And embrace life in a playful way.

Thundering within,
Emotions reveal the truth,
Acceptance is key.

Absolute Acceptance

I meditated and wondered,
Can I release this tightness without losing openness?
Both anxiety and excitement in my body thundered.

With no agenda or outcome, I pondered,
No need to fix or heal these feelings, no duress.
I meditated and wondered.

Motivated to change, I controlled and surrendered,
Emoting something pleasant, my mind did assess.
Both anxiety and excitement in my body thundered.

What if I dropped these thoughts, no longer encumbered,
Who would I be in these sensations, without distress?
I meditated and wondered.

I sought happiness in my body, no longer outnumbered,
My vessel is a part of me, but not myself, I confess.
Both anxiety and excitement in my body thundered.

Embracing all my emotions, a truth uncovered,
Absolute acceptance is key to joy and progress.

I meditated and wondered,
Both anxiety and excitement in my body thundered.

Peaceful downtime calms,
Reflection recharges the mind,
Rest should not be missed.

Mindful Downtime

In the pursuit of life's endless race,
We often forget to slow down our pace,
Playful activities and some downtime,
Are key to keep our mental health just fine.

In moments of fun, we discover joy,
Creativity and spontaneity we employ,
Stress is reduced, our mood is lifted high,
Well-being enhanced, as we laugh and sigh.

With mindful downtime, there's space to rest,
To reflect, recharge, and give our minds a test,
In a world that's fast-paced, easy to neglect,
The importance of rest, we shouldn't reject.

Vacations or meditation, minutes, or an hour,
Helps to reduce stress, and regain our power,
Boosting our productivity, raising creativity,
The perfect play time with kids, the best activity.

Let's not forget the value they bring,
To our mental health, let's give them a fling,
For without these breaks, we risk losing sight,
Of the joy of living, and the beauty of life's light.

Release the old self,
Step forward with faith and trust,
Awakened and free.

Belief System

*We mourn the loss of beliefs, old way of being,
The comfort of what we knew,
the familiar way of seeing.*

*But in this elegy, we honor the death of the old,
And embrace the birth of the new,
a story yet to be told.*

*Let's release what no longer serves us,
And step into the unknown
with faith, trust, and purpose.*

*For as we shed the layers of our past,
We uncover our true selves at last.*

*May we navigate this transition with grace,
And awaken to a new world, a new space.*

*Where love, unity, and oneness reside,
And our spirits soar, free and alive.*

Old beliefs bind tight,
Our spirit breaks us free,
Joy and wonder reign.

Nature of Spirit

This is an ode to the nature of our spirit,
That guides us on our life's journey,
With signs that energize and uplift,
Leading us down paths, like a gurney.

It's easy to fall into addictive patterns,
And numb ourselves to life's true call,
But our spirit calls us to be transparent,
And to always remain honest with all.

With an open and receptive heart,
We can align with the qualities of spirit,
And flow with the manifested reality,
So, we can truly thrive and flourish in it.

Yet sometimes we're held back by beliefs,
Rigid and unyielding, they can bind us tight,
But with the help of spirit, we can break free,
And live in a state of joyful, wondrous delight.

Stress smothers my soul,
Time to bloom and reinvent,
No more exhaustion.

Strength of the Warrior

The shackles of the past are undone,
No longer in darkness, now in the sun.

I stand tall with newfound strength,
A warrior of light, going to any length.

The obtrusive thoughts no longer control,
I have regained my body and soul.

With clarity and focus, I walk my path,
No longer fearing the aftermath.

The darkness that once consumed me,
Has now dissipated, and I am free.

When the stress of my persona smothers,
It's time to reinvent, bloom like flowers.

I live each day with purpose and light,
No longer exhausted by the night.

I am grateful for the lessons learned,
As my spirit persists to be affirmed.

Love despite flaws there,
No need for overthinking,
Find thrill in the mess.

Beauty of Imperfection

Life is a journey, complex and rough,
Filled with emotions, weaves, and turns,
Easy to get lost in the messiness,
Feeling uncertain and overwhelmed.

Our self-worth sometimes lies in others,
Unhealthy coping mechanisms ensue,
But embracing imperfections,
We see splendor in what's askew.

Loving ourselves despite flaws,
Finding freedom in vulnerability,
We're all imperfect beings,
It's okay to be down occasionally.

Let's live in the moment, not overthinking,
Celebrating the beauty of imperfection,
For it's often in the messy times,
That we find the most thrill and connection.

Dark and light merged,
Wholeness embraced, taking flight,
Free to flow and grow.

Shadow Integration

Upon my journey of self-discovery,
I faced my shadows with curiosity,
Uncovering anxious parts within,
And embracing discomfort they bring.

Through my deep soul introspection,
I observed the darkness and connection,
To the hidden forces within me,
And the sacred light that helps me see.

Though it may be difficult to face,
I befriend my anxiety with grace,
Knowing it's a necessity for growth,
To transcend the limitations, I know.

By integrating the dark into light,
I embrace my wholeness and take flight,
Less polarized, I'm free to flow,
In life's ups and downs, what a show!

The key to joy is
staying present in each hour,
Gaining strength, life's best power.

Present Moment

Let me revel in the simple things I see,
The gentle sway of trees and soft breeze,
Colors of the sky, a bird's sweet melody,
And the peace that comes with passing ease.

Let me cherish every moment that I live,
And find my happiness in the present hour,
For only in this way can I truly give,
Gaining strength to face life's greatest power.

So let me live my life with open eyes,
And take each moment as it comes to me,
For in this way, I'll find a life that satisfies,
And learn to be the best that I can be.

Through mystic paths, I've noticed a way,
A better version of myself, simple sway.

As sovereign beings,
We create authentic life,
Transmuting shadows.

True Essence

I shed the layers of societal conditioning,
Allowing my inner voice to guide my vision.
No more seeking external validation,
My power comes from my internal sensation.

I embrace my shadow self with love and grace,
Transmuting darkness into light with every trace.
I honor my past and the lessons it taught,
But I release the pain that it brought.

I am a sovereign being, free from fear,
Creating a life that feels authentic and clear.
With each breath, I expand my consciousness,
Living in alignment with my true essence.

I am grateful for the journey that led me here,
With an open heart, I face each new frontier.
Trusting in the universe to guide my way,
I am divinely supported, every single day.

Stress of negative
Thoughts trigger an imbalance,
Manage reactions.

Emotional Wellness

Amidst my forties, I discovered a truth,
That feelings held a weight on my affairs,
Affecting my relationships and my youth,
And even mental health beyond repairs.

But as time passed, my reactions evolve,
My emotional wellness grew, improved,
Adapted to the stresses, I could solve,
And setbacks I endured, quickly removed.

My negative emotions now so few,
My resilience developed day by day,
With coping strategies aiding me through,
In healthy ways, my tension would fade away.

For stress, a double-edged sword, did teach,
The misaligned body can't function, preach.

In profound slumber,
our bodies find the release,
To rise refreshed, full of peace.

Power of Sleep

In calming sleep, I find sweet solace there,
For body and mind, it's a vital need,
Fatigue unrelenting, a burden to bear,
A mountain of weariness, hard to exceed.

With proper rest, I gain much clarity,
My thoughts are focused, mind is clear,
My actions grow with purpose, surety,
When well-rested, weariness won't tear.

Let's not neglect this treasure, this boon,
A nightly balm that soothes our care,
For though it may seem simple, too soon,
The benefits we reap are truly rare.

In deep slumber, our bodies find release,
And rise refreshed, renewed, and full of peace.

Grief is a cruel beast,
Emitting shadows that feast,
With fangs, toils, and flares.

Coping with Grief

My world was shattered the day she passed,
The dreams of the beloved laid to rest.
The loss of my dear grandmother, so vast,
A void of an angel, a wound in my chest.

Grief is a vicious beast that toils and flares,
Emitting the shadows that feast with fangs,
Squeezing my heart till it bleeds and tears,
Draining me of all my mortal pangs.

In sorrow's grip, I find no respite,
As grief's cruel claws dig deep within,
Each breath a struggle, each flash a fight,
Against the pain that never seems to thin.

The weight of loss is a heavy load,
A burden that I cannot bear alone,
For every step feels like a treacherous road,
And every memory a sharpened stone.

But in the depths of sorrow's darkest night,
A flicker of hope, a glimmer of light,
A reminder that her love still burns bright,
And that in time, my heart will take flight.

I know in my sadness, I will soon find,
A comfort in the memories we shared,
For they will stay with me until the end,
A testament to love that never fades.

In this darkness, I found a ray of light,
A hope that shone amidst the deepest night.

Hold on to the love,
As we say farewell to loss,
Carry them inside.

In Honour

When we mourn the loss of someone dear,
A pain that cuts so deep and makes us fear,
The emptiness that fills our broken hearts,
As we come to terms with what now departs.

We mourn the loss of what we held so tight,
The dreams we shared, the hopes so bright,
Memories we shared with those we held dear,
The festivities we'll cherish year after year.

The pain of loss is hard to comprehend,
A wound that seems to never truly mend,
We search for answers in the depths of grief,
It's any angry brute that needs some relief.

But in this time of darkness and of sorrow,
We must remember that a new tomorrow,
Will come again, and with hope will rise,
As we learn to cope without loved ones' eyes.

Though we may never understand the why,
We hold onto the love that will never die,
And as we say goodbye to what we've lost,
We find strength to carry them inside, no cost.

So let us mourn, and let us weep and cry,
And honor those we've lost with tears that dry,
For though they may be gone, they still remain,
In memories and love that will forever sustain.

A practice that's old,
Relevant as life unfolds,
Live in mindful space.

Being Mindful

Come hither, friends, and listen to my tale,
Of mindfulness, a practice that shall prevail,
In moments still, we find our inner peace,
And with each breath, troubles start to cease.

It's a practice that is ages old,
But still relevant, as life unfolds,
For in our busy lives, we often forget,
The simple joy of living, without regret.

To be present in this moment, with full intent,
And embrace what life has to offer, content,
To let go of worries, future or past,
And cherish every moment, that won't last.

Oh mindfulness, how wonderful thou art,
A practice that can heal both mind and heart,
So let us all embrace this gift with grace,
And live each day, in a mindful space.

The darkness consumed,
Whispers of unknown ghouls near,
But my strength prevailed.

The Haunting

In Minori's night, a battle was fought,
Against the darkness, and all it wrought,
Unknown ghouls beckoned my soul,
To take me down to an abyssal hole.

The fear did not consume my mind,
For with strength and light combined,
I battled for hours against the dark,
And held steadfast, the horrors embark.

My past had kept me blind to the truth,
Of the darkness lurking in my youth,
But now, in Minori's embrace,
I faced the horror with unyielding grace.

With every strike and every blow,
I fought against the unknown foe,
And though the blackness clung to me,
I never let it take me down completely.

The journey was long and hard,
Leaving me battered and scarred,
But through every battle and every test,
I emerged victorious, stronger, blessed.

Now I stand before the abyssal gate,
Mourning the loss of an ego once great,
But through the darkness and the fight,
I emerged victorious with my inner light.

Inner devotion,
Is the flow of energy,
A journey of growth.

Line of Enquiry

In the stillness of my mind, I reflect,
The power of my thoughts, and their effect,
On my life and well-being, so profound,
And the suffering that they have often found.

I have learned that thoughts can be a cage,
A trap that keeps me stuck in endless rage,
And as I let go of this mental weight,
I find a sense of peace that is so great.

What's the process to release this hold,
To let go beliefs that make me so cold.
I have adopted a line of inquiry,
A progressive approach to set me free.

By working with my body, mind, and soul,
I trace myself back into awareness whole,
And find a baseline knowledge of trauma,
That helps me heal when I learn from karma.

It's a process that's not roused by projection,
And washes away my stress and my affliction,
Removing cause and effect, with gentle motion,
So, I can investigate each moment, with affection.

Within each instant, eternal life is grand,
And in accepting discomfort, I understand,
That it flows as energy in motion,
A journey of growth, and inner devotion.

Recognize value,
Of nervous system preserved,
Without self-judgment.

Trauma Thriver

Moving forward in life seemed out of reach,
As if each step were burdened by a weight.
Futility and hopelessness in equal measure
Made it difficult to see a better fate.

But I knew I needed to break this cycle,
And so, I started with a tiny change.
Just a shift in the direction I wanted,
To create the life that felt less strange.

Leaning into the choices I made,
And embracing the life that I deserved,
I stopped judging my nervous system,
And recognized the value it preserved.

Releasing the self-blame and judgments,
I knew in my heart, I did the best that I could.
Despite the bad things that had happened,
I survived, a warrior of light, no falsehood.

Now I take it one day at a time,
Knowing I'm doing my best to thrive.
Believing in myself makes the difference,
And I'm grateful to be truly alive.

The truth is in breath,
Free from the Karmic cycles,
Of fear, suffering.

My Truth

*My truth is anything that sets me free,
Thoughts, actions, or viewpoints
that elicit total relaxation in my body
A state of balance and sovereignty.*

*These qualities are not of fear or division,
Like deception that hurts and betrays.
My truth can only comfort and liberate,
With endless mercy, my innocent is at peace.*

*Only resistance to reality causes me pain
Spiraling out of control from the strain.
But when I speak with pure intentions,
I hold space for your truth, not harming another.*

*This vulnerability supports my essence,
And the knowing encoded within blossoms,
To manifest my natural state of being,
as I open up to love of self with authority.*

*My truth is in every breath I take,
nourishing the hunger of my crystal heart.
It is a freedom from the never-ending chaos,
The Karmic cycle of anguish and suffering.*

*My truth enables me to contribute
to humanity's conscious evolution.
It is the physical representation
of my higher self from the loving
expression of Divine that I AM.*

Setting boundaries,
Allowing the natural flow,
Letting go of force.

Setting Boundaries

*Oh, the power of attraction,
Guiding me through life's reactions.
A force so strong, yet gentle too,
Leading me to experiences anew.*

*I don't chase, I simply allow,
The universe to show me how,
To attract people, places, and things,
That align with the vibration my soul sings.*

*In this way, I erect boundaries firm,
Against those who may cause harm.
Real connection honors diverse views,
And with gratitude, my light ensues.*

*My inspiration is mine to choose,
Respecting boundaries as I cruise.
I won't allow anyone to invade,
My energy and time, a precious trade.*

*For the unhealed, my existence may offend,
But their actions do not define or bend,
My will to choose who I will be,
In this space, I am sovereign and free.*

*If they can't meet me in this sacred place,
It's an invitation for trust and grace.
Found within my electric heart so true,
The power of attraction, leading me to you.*

Tears of peaceful bliss,
Rose in complete awe, witness,
Ascend, angel wings.

Higher Realms

Oh, Ravello, you have shown me the way,
To embrace my true essence, day by day,
And awaken my inner angel's flight,
To soar with Divine in unending delight.

Your beauty and tranquility,
Have touched my heart so deeply,
Infusing me with magnetic energy,
And lighting my path to destiny.

You are a portal to higher realms,
A gateway to unseen helms,
Where the veil of shadow is lifted,
And the true self is revealed, gifted.

Oh, Ravello, I give thanks to thee,
For opening my eyes to see,
The sacred light within my being,
And my purpose of divine meaning.

May your beauty and energy,
Guide and inspire us endlessly,
To awaken our true potential,
And shine our starlight essential.

Be accountable,
For emotions that trigger,
Releasing patterns.

Walking My Path

To live in peace, harmony, gratitude, and joy,
Is the aim of my life, as I journey through,
I've learned the harm of projecting and reacting,
Of getting defensive, losing my karmic points anew.

I now take responsibility for my triggers,
And work to release the patterns that bind,
Through positive intentions and mindful actions,
I boost my vibrational frequency, with love in mind.

The universe rewards pure and honest energy,
No faking or pretending can ever pass,
I embrace the lessons that fuel my evolution,
Committed to walking my true path at last.

Agony grips tight,
Twisting my heart with its might,
Grace and light in sight.

Morning Breaks

In dreams I see a world of grace and light,
Where love abounds and pain is cast away,
But morning breaks and brings the endless fight.

When agony grips me like a vise,
The pain twists and turns within my heart,
In dreams I see a world of grace and light.

But life is filled with struggles and plight,
And even love can wither and decay,
As morning breaks and brings the endless fight.

The darkness looms, chasing out the sight,
And worry and doubt leads my heart astray,
In dreams I see a world of grace and light.

It lingers on like some dark paradise,
A love that tears my world and soul apart.
As morning breaks and brings the endless fight.

For though the world may test me with its might,
I hold on to my truth that guides my way,
In dreams I see a world of grace and light,
But morning breaks and brings the endless fight.

Guiding voice amassed,
Found peace with self-discipline,
Importance of care.

Guiding Voice

In my life, my focus was always on the task,
Ignoring the feelings that I had within,
But I've learned the value of self-care at last.

To find balance, I had to take on the big ask,
Prioritizing well-being with discipline,
In my life, my focus was always on the task.

Reflection showed the gaps that I had to unmask,
Emotional, physical, mental states to begin,
But I've learned the value of self-care at last.

Mastering my thoughts and banishing the mask,
Setting my intentions with the power to win,
In my life, my focus was always on the task.

Muting the distractions, my guiding voice amassed,
A newfound peace with self-discipline to within,
But I've learned the importance of self-care at last.

Embracing this new rhythm, inner work is a must,
Boundaries with clarity, this life I will begin,
In my life, my focus was always on the task,
But I've learned the value of self-care at last.

Writing, painting, play,
Games for the soul, healing's aim,
A cure truly grand.

Artistic Creation

There once was a therapy so grand,
With healing powers that spanned the land,
Artistic creation was its name,
Writing, painting, playing its game,
A cure for the soul, so truly grand.

Embrace fire's glow,
Firmly grip pockets of peace,
Best self I can show.

Honouring My Spirit

When I'm not feeling motivated,
The universe shifts me into a higher state,
So long as I'm open to transcending,
And welcoming divine guidance's elate.

No longer held back by routine and habits,
I honor my spirit and let go of the finite,
Clearing my emotions, I release resistance,
Accepting my needs, not just what's in sight.

I set my intentions through action and flow,
Beyond my physical self and all that I aspire,
Reconnecting with my innate sense of wholeness,
And embracing the power of my divine fire.

Firmly gripping onto pockets of peace,
I was finally the best version of me,
Love is about giving our heart,
With no expectations of thee.

Deep cave, I reside,
Welcoming transformation,
Gifts of growth inside.

Inner Cave

In the depths of an inner cave I dwell,
Not running, nor hiding, just simply being,
Welcoming all that arises, to dispel.

With each passing moment, I can tell,
The gift of transformation is freeing,
In the depths of an inner cave, I dwell.

Let this space heal, don't let it pass or quell,
Embrace the burn, alchemy that's freeing,
Welcoming all that arises, to dispel.

For in this stillness, all pain can excel,
And joy can dance with equal footing,
In the depths of an inner cave, I dwell.

From the ashes of past, a new self-propels,
Awakened, alive, and always seeing,
Welcoming all that arises, to dispel.

So let this space be a sacred temple,
Of growth, of healing, of limitless being,
In the depths of an inner cave I dwell,
Welcoming all that arises, to dispel.

Living in balance,
Choosing energy wisely,
Honoring my path.

Co-Creating Reality

To live in harmony, I choose energy wisely,
And honor my journey, accepting what it holds.
I recognize my pain and let go of what doesn't serve,
And step into my power, taking control of my soul.
The universe flows through me, guiding my path,
As I trust in the journey and let go of the past.

With an open heart, I embrace every lesson,
And find purpose in the connections I make.
I let my light shine, and I honor my essence,
As I move through this life with love, not hate.

With each step I take, I am guided by grace,
I co-create my reality of divine's master plan.
Grateful for every encounter and challenge I face,
For they have shaped me into the person I am.

A calm lullaby,
Darkness fills the sky with ease,
As the sun sets free.

Time Does Fly

The sun sets, and darkness fills the sky,
As stars above begin to twinkle bright.
Another day is gone, the time does fly.

The moon shines on, a tranquil lullaby,
And all the beings rest throughout the night.
The sun sets, and darkness fills the sky.

We all must live, love, laugh and cry,
Make the most of every precious sight.
Another day is gone, the time does fly.

The moments pass, and soon we say goodbye,
To all the things we held with all our might.
The sun sets, and darkness fills the sky.

But in our hearts, the memories won't die,
Reminding us we too shall rise, shine light.
Another day is gone, the time does fly.

So let us cherish every moment nigh,
And live each day with all our soul's delight.
The sun sets, and darkness fills the sky.
Another day is gone, the time does fly.

Nature's canvas vast,
Hues of every shade and kind,
Soul resounds in awe.

Coloured Lens

I realized my belief shaped my reality,
A truth that once was hidden from my sight,
The power of thought, a force of vitality.

But then I learned to let the labels go,
To see beyond the surface, brings clarity,
This colored lens brings wisdom, I know.

I used to judge experiences as good or bad,
But now I embrace space for transformation,
Without wallowing in dread and feeling sad.

I was summoned to a place of vivid creation,
Where both demons and angels coexist,
And though initiation was a scary situation,
I emerged with wings beyond the veil's mist.

With every passing grade, I learned life skills,
Permitting emotions to flow like a sieve,
My colored lens had cleansed blind spots' ills.

Through quiet contemplation, I find insight,
As stars twinkle in a symphony of sound,
And I am filled with wonder and delight.

Nature's beauty, all around me, abounds,
A canvas painted with hues of every kind,
And in its presence, my soul resounds.

The world is vast, and yet, in my mind,
I find a place of peace and harmony,
Where troubles fade, and joy is what I find.

In the gentle breeze,
I surrender to the flow,
Crashing waves recede.

State of Flow

There's a technique I heard to calm fear,
To silence anxiety, that's always near,
Visual centering became my guide,
A new perspective to view the worldwide.

When in flight or fight mode I have found,
I centered my focus, feet on the ground,
Away from external chaos and strife,
My seat of awareness, center of life.

As I watched myself in this peaceful state,
The paranoia began to abate,
I became the witness of my own fear,
And felt my instinct begin to appear.

In this surrender, stress was silenced,
Guidance from my higher-self enhanced,
My intuition grew, clear and bright,
As I entered life's flow of delight.

Dormant powers within me came alive,
As I learned to self-regulate and thrive,
The flow state of life's alignment I found,
Through visual centering, peace all around.

Space for diffusion,
Attuned to the universe,
Discernment unveiled.

Melting the Untruth

I adopted a theory, we're born a blank slate,
This infinite potential removed negative trait.
In this nothingness, all prospects unlocked,
I learned to co-design, my life unblocked.

When my spirit was filled with fallacies,
It misaligned my perspective, a paralysis.
With every breath I reoriented my path,
A long windy road perplexed by wrath.

Emptying my cup of all delusions,
I made space for the organic diffusion.
Becoming attuned as the universal sleuth,
I developed discernment melting the untruth.

Echoes from my soul,
Beacon of light in despair,
A force we can share.

Creating My Legacy

My purpose transcends the physical plane,
As I tap into the endless well of inspiration.
I transmit the divine essence that flows within,
Weaving words to awaken and inspire creation.

With each stroke of the pen, I unleash a new realm,
Bringing to life a legacy that croons in my mind.
I paint pictures with phrases, evoking emotions,
A tapestry of poetry, one stroke of a kind.

My voice echoes with the depths of my soul,
A beacon of light in a world of dark despair.
Offering hope to those lost in confusion,
Guiding towards a life beyond compare.

For in the realm of the written word,
There lies a power beyond compare.
It transforms, it heals, it unites,
A force of love that we all can share.

So, I continue to write, to create, to inspire,
And let my soul dance upon the page.
For in this act of pure expression,
I find freedom, joy, and a timeless stage.

About the Author

Lali A. Love is a multi-genre, award-winning author and bestseller of dark fantasy, science fiction, paranormal thriller, and metaphysical poetry.

Since July 2019, she has published her Amazon best-selling novels Heart of a Warrior Angel: From Darkness to Light, and her first series, The De-Coding of Jo, Blade of Truth, and Keys to Eternity.

Lali also released a coffee table artbook with inspirational poetry, The Joy of I.T. (Infinite Transcendence), as well as Organic eMotions: Poetry for hUmaNITY.

She has received the NYC Big Book Award in Poetry Anthology, a Global e-Book Gold Award, the Elite Choice Gold Award, the Book of Excellence Award, the Queer Indie Lit Youth Gold Award, the Global Book Award, and the International Reader's Favorite Gold Award for quality and powerful storytelling.

Her mission is to empower, enlighten, and entertain her readers by bridging the concepts of metaphysics with gripping storytelling and uplifting poetry.

Lali aspires to write stimulating, thought-provoking, and relevant character-based novels that relate to modern-day issues and invoke an emotional response in her readers.

As an intuitive, alchemist, and energy healer, Lali intends to help elevate levels of consciousness by shining the light on sensitive subject matter to assist individuals in their healing journeys. She is an advocate for self-love, vulnerability, authentic truths, equality, diversity, unity, freedom, women, and children.

www.ingramcontent.com/pod-product-compliance
Lightning Source LLC
Chambersburg PA
CBHW020526080526
44583CB00013B/754